In Sorrow and In Joy

In Sorrow and In Joy

D. E. YOUNG

RESOURCE *Publications* • Eugene, Oregon

IN SORROW AND IN JOY

Copyright © 2012 D. E. Young. All rights reserved. Except for brief quotations in critical publications or reviews, no part of this book may be reproduced in any manner without prior written permission from the publisher. Write: Permissions, Wipf and Stock Publishers, 199 W. 8th Ave., Suite 3, Eugene, OR 97401.

Resource Publications
An imprint of Wipf and Stock Publishers
199 W. 8th Ave., Suite 3
Eugene, OR 97401

www.wipfandstock.com

isbn 13: 978-1-61097-821-7

Manufactured in the U.S.A.

Contents

Foreword / xiii
Preface / xv

George's Song / 1
Letters / 1
Chastisement / 2
"We Wrestle Not Against Flesh and Blood" / 2
Vintage / 3
Affliction / 3
Confession / 4
Psalm 119:57ff / 4
Isaiah 50:4 / 4
Husbandry / 5
Anticipation / 6
Recompense / 7
Election / 7
Meribah / 7
Lamentations 3 / 8
Psalm 88 / 9
White Stone / 11
Job / 11
Isaiah 12 / 13
White Robe / 14
Job (II) / 14

Contents

Untitled / 15
Grace / 15
Hope / 15
For Joel / 16
Meditation / 16
At The Table / 17
Paradox / 17
Computers and Creation / 17
After Long Illness / 18
Drought / 18
Romans 8:26 / 18
Fruitfulness / 19
On Election Day / 19
Longing / 20
Maranatha / 20
On The Feast / 21
Confidence / 21
Assurance / 21
For a Lady Who is Ill / 21
For My Brother / 22
Affliction (II) / 22
On the Marriage of a Widow With Children /22
Affliction (III) / 22
On The Death of an Elder / 23
Psalm 116 / 23
Purification / 24
Fear / 25
On Stony Ground / 25
Bitterness / 25
Sweetness / 25
Habakkuk 3 / 26

Contents

On The Opening of a New Place of Worship / 27
In Doubting Castle / 28
The Thanksgiving / 28
Psalm 141 / 28
Humility / 29
Hebrews 6:19 / 29
The Whisper / 30
Aleph / 30
Psalm 142 / 30
Beth / 31
Petition / 32
On Sincerity / 32
Perseverance / 32
On The Rebuke / 33
Psalm 6 / 33
Again / 34
Thanksgiving 35/
On a Word Shot From a Distance / 35
Humility (II) / 36
Fall / 36
Winter / 36
Spring / 36
Summer / 37
Micah 7 / 37
Balaam / 39
Refuge / 39
Perspective (II) / 40
Gimel / 40
He / 40
Job (III) / 41
For Graduation from a Faithful Seminary / 41

vii

Contents

Magdalene / 42
Obedience (For Bear) / 43
Enlightenment / 43
On Princeton Chapel / 43
Affliction (IV) / 44
Mark 5:28 / 44
Manasseh / 45
Shame / 45
On Nearly Nine Years in the Pew / 45
Chastisement (II) / 46
Grace (II) / 46
To My Shepherds / 46
Submission / 47
Mordecai's Song / 47
Resistance / 47
Confession (II) / 47
Rest / 48
Chastisement (III) / 48
From Job 36 / 48
Healing / 49
Fear (II) / 49
To My Physician / 50
On His Manhood / 50
Communion Meditation / 50
Expectation / 52
Incarnation / 52
Psalm 121 / 52
Psalm 43 / 53
On His Fetters
On the Church Gathering for Worship / 54
Extra Verses for Psalm 42 as Set in the Trinity Hymnal /54

Contents

Invocation / 55
Hardening / 55
Baptism / 56
Baptism (II) / 56
On Aging / 57
At Interpreter's House / 57
At Interpreter's House (II) / 57
Forgiveness / 58
Longing (II) / 58
On the Mystery of Providence / 58
Psalm 4 / 59
If Thou Canst / 59
On Her Darkness / 60
On Death and Dying / 60
Burnt at the Stake / 60
On a Glass of Wine in the Evening / 60
Trust / 61
Eliezer / 61
Ebenezer / 61
From Deuteronomy / 62
For a Ruling Elder / 62
Nabal / 63
For Pastor On His 50th Birthday / 63
To My Manager / 63
To Pastor, in His Illness / 64
To the Watkins Family (With Thanks) / 64
Restoration / 64
On the Death of Lady, a Standard Poodle / 65
Michal / 65
Thanks (II) / 66
With Thanks / 66

Contents

Widow's Mite / 66
On Losing My House to Foreclosure / 67
Words / 67
Jonah / 68
Dismay / 68
Puppies / 68
On Bunhill Fields / 68
Penitence / 69
At the Table (II) / 69
On the Baptism of Carl Vos Watkins / 70
We Have a Great High Priest / 70
On Dental Work and Silence / 71
On the Death of a Deacon / 71
For Irena Sandler / 71
Jesus Wept / 72
On the Death of Ed Minor / 72
On the Death of Shell Regan / 73
On Anderson Manor / 74
On the Sacrifice of Isaac / 74
For the Deacons / 75
On the Death of S. L. / 76
Naomi / 76
Solitude / 77
Ravens / 78
Sustained by a Widow / 78
From Proverbs 31 / 79
From Romans 15 / 80
On Human Opinion / 81
To Our Lord, Jesus Christ / 81
On the Anger of Jesus Christ / 81
Dust / 82

Contents

A Secret Princess / 82
In Contemplation of a Dying Saint / 83
For Jack, on the Occasion of His Death / 84
For Marjorie Paauwe, on the Occasion of Her Death / 84
For a Pharisee, in Contemplation of Her Death / 86
On Being a Woman / 87
Death's Invitation / 87
Another Take on Childhood Songs: Jesus Loves Me / 87
Another Take on Childhood Songs: Jesus Loves
 the Little Children / 88
Blind Bartimaeus / 88
From Numbers 16 / 89
From Exodus 33 and Romans 3 / 90
My Burka / 90
The Command / 91
On the Refusal of a Friend to Repent / 91
"But With Most of Them, He was not Well-Pleased" / 92
On the Death of Gabriella Valente / 93
Dwelling in Tents With Abraham, Isaac, and Jacob / 94
On Yet Another Average Review / 94
On The Prayed For Conversion of a Friend / 95
On My Nephew's Wedding / 96
God is a Man of War / 97
Resurrection / 97
On "One Ocean," a Song Heard at Sea World® / 98
On Psalm 8, Hebrews 2, and Sea World® / 99
On Luke 16 / 99
Ambition / 100
Comfort / 100
Two Hands / 100
On Seeing a Rainbow / 101

Contents

Welcome to the Church / 101
Grace is a Flower / 102
A Man of Sorrows / 102
Three Shipwrecks / 103
Mary and Martha / 103
Why? / 103
Jericho / 103
On the Marriage of Two Friends / 104
On a Couple Being Reunited in Marriage / 105
On Christian Liberty / 105
I John 4:7–8 / 106
Ambition II / 106

Foreword

POETRY DATES FROM ANTIQUITY and continues through the centuries. The poems of King David speak with the same power, as they did a millennium before Christ. We still are touched by the truth and nobility of the seventeenth-century work of Anne Bradstreet.

Where have the great poets gone?

The volume before us, *In Sorrow and in Joy*, demonstrates that the days of great poets have not departed.

Dorothy Young draws upon several resources in the composition of her book. There is her faith commitment. Like David, she acknowledges her ultimate allegiance: "O LORD my God, in you I have taken refuge" (Psalm 7:1). There is her degree in English literature from Bryan College. There are her many years of careful study of the Bible and theology. There is her gift of eloquence granted by the Holy Spirit.

There is more, however, than these things. Like David of old, Dorothy writes out of a wide range of life experience. She has known unspeakable sorrow and exhilarating exuberance. There have been moments of anxiety and also the peace that passes all understanding.

God has equipped her to write poems that mirror the experiences of her soul, but also the experiences of all the people of God.

The volume before us instructs our minds, moves our emotions, and teaches us how to live.

Do you seek wisdom, as one seeks for silver and hidden treasures?

Take up and read.

Mark J. Larson

Preface

CONTRARY TO SOME TEACHINGS that have achieved popularity in recent years, the Christian's life in this world is not unmixed joy, peace, ease, and enjoyment. God's people have always met with trial, anguish, distress, pain, and suffering, as well as with the great delight of knowing and worshipping God and enjoying His people's companionship.

The Christian in affliction should not think that he is the first of the Lord's people to pass this way. Scripture records not only the joys of Christianity but also the woe that sometimes comes upon God's people, which is sent, as is the joy, by the loving hand of a faithful Father for reasons that are not always immediately apparent. Our Father in Heaven always works the events of our lives for His glory and the good of His Church, whether the experience is pleasant or unpleasant for us at the time.

It is my hope and prayer that this little volume will be an encouragement to the Lord's people, whether they find themselves in present affliction or enjoying "green pastures" and "still waters."

George's Song

Weep not for me as here I lie
or in the earth my dust they place.
My soul leaps up with boundless joy
because I look upon His face.
My body sleeps a little while
but soon shall throb with life again
and, perfect, join my happy soul.
I'll dance for joy before Him then.
Restored the image of my God
both soul and body then shall be,
and with my Lord Who flesh did wear
I'll worship God with ecstasy.
Long though the night of weeping be,
do not forget 'tis soon gone by.
My hope, my confidence is this,
that Jesus lives . . . and so shall I.
Awake! The silver trumpet calls.
Come serve the Lord with godly fear.
The night's far spent, the day's at hand,
and Jesus shortly shall appear.

Letters

What strange love letters Thou dost send!
What sweet, harsh words that breaking mend.
To comfort me, Thou dost reprove.
Thy rod's the earnest of Thy love.
That Thy blows be not misspent
grant me grace now to repent.

Chastisement

Lord, You're coming with Your rod.
I fear and shake before my God
for You will smite me, this I know,
and well-deserved is every blow.
Yet, Lord, in smiting, break me not.
I'm Your bruised reed; O quench me not,
Your smoking flax, for You did say
though You chastise me every day
that You will make me all Your own
and that although You make me groan
my Jesus' blessed face I'll see
in perfect joy and purity.
Lord, let the strokes fall where they may,
but let their blueness cleanse away
that which provoked Your holy ire
and purge my heart with secret fire.

"We Wrestle Not Against Flesh and Blood"

Homewards I tread with leaden step
and with a heavy heart.
Before me now, I see my foe
armed with a fiery dart.
How can a man an angel fight?
I shall be overthrown!
But see! One comes for my defense.
It is the Stronger Man.
No power in earth or heaven can stay
the motion of His hand.
Now I can struggle on with hope,
for I am not alone.
Courage, my soul; you shall be safe
and stand before His throne.

In Sorrow and In Joy

Vintage

My precious Lord, Your table's spread
with holy wine and sacred bread,
sweet fruits of grace for all to see,
but You will not yet sup with me.
Your wine is good, well-tempered, old.
Two thousand years has lain, 'tis told,
in dungeon dark and palace bright,
Celestial vintage, clear and light.
'Twas new made in that bitter hour,
the winepress of God's angry power.
You said You would not taste it till
You come the promise to fulfill.
See now, my Lord, 'tis ripe and sweet.
Come with Your angels round Your feet.
Come, taste the fruit of Your own love,
and our infirmity remove.

Affliction

My God is King of Kings alone.
He works all things at will
and will not cast my soul away
but His own oath fulfill.
He leads me through the valley dark;
my feeble heart would fail
if I had not an Advocate
within the holy veil.
I would have perished in my woe
had not His Word made plain
He'll rescue me when He sees fit,
stretch out His arm again.
He does not willingly afflict
nor chide the sons of men.

When He has worked His holy will
I shall have peace again.
Some day He'll ease my weary soul
and give me a new song.
But till that day my spirit sighs,
"My Sovereign Lord, how long?"

Confession

I do not wish to own my sin
lest I should mar my name.
But You, who had no cause to blush,
hid not Your face from shame.

Psalm 119:57ff

Whether You lead through inky night
or by a sweet, bright, pleasant way,
hereto I set my hand, heart, feet:
my God, I will obey.
Grant me Your gracious favor, Lord;
I know that You are mine.
I will take heed to all Your Words
for You are King divine.
Then shall I keep my heart with fear
because Your eye is fixed on me.
I'll run within Your ways, my God.
Grant grace that it may be.

Isaiah 50:4

You have the tongue of learning, Lord;
now give my heart a willing ear.
Sustain my weary soul with words,

my inner man with comfort clear.
No other words are like Your Word;
none else has all-creating power,
dividing soul and spirit, sharp,
heart-searching, living every hour.
My words are weak, and swiftly gone
their lingering echo dies away.
Your Word is steadfast set in heaven;
each jot and tittle waits the Day.
Here is Your love (no tongue can frame)
and all Your holy, matchless ways.
No man can hold a candle to
the Son's eternal, piercing rays.
I have seen truth (it is Your Word),
and handled mysteries veiled in light.
How long before Your will is done
and faith becomes unclouded sight?

Husbandry

You furrowed up my stony heart
and planted there Your precious seed.
You gave a rich and plenteous light,
and living water for my need.
Alas, I did not strictly watch.
The rising plants began to drop.
And cold neglect and careless ease
now threaten to destroy the crop.
Your tender plants require much care
to grow in such a wasteland, Lord.
I must arise and tend them well,
but weeds grow of their own accord.

In Sorrow and In Joy

Anticipation

"For we shall all be made manifest
before the judgment seat of Christ."

Thick clouds are darkly gathering;
the wind is rising too.
The shadows lengthen all around,
the day is almost through.
I hear the thunder far away,
I see the lightning flash,
and down below upon the shore
the rising breakers crash.
I dread the storm that's coming now,
but welcome it as well.
The earth is waiting breathlessly,
the outcome who can tell?
The Judge is now approaching;
before the doors He stands.
I have not seen my Advocate,
but in His mighty hands
is graved my name indelible.
Upon the bench He waits.
Christ Jesus is the Righteous Judge
Who also pleads my case.
My sins are hundreds, thousands—
no, they're many, many more.
But He Who judges also knows the penalty He bore.
And when my day in court has come
and the appointed hour,
I must be sheltered in the Rock
from judgment's fiery shower.
And since no other storm will rage
like this, the very last,
in Him I'll hide myself and wait

until the clouds are past.
Soon comes the sweet and dreadful day
although I know not when.
But this I know, when Him I see
my weariness shall end.

Recompense

By faith I see the great reward;
the holy city fair.
In her the King of Glory dwells,
and many saints are there.
He is the pearl of greatest price!
Worth more than life to me.
And I will cast away my toys,
O lovely Christ, for Thee!

Election

To show Thy strength to every saint,
Thou choosest, Lord, the weak and faint.
To show Thy purifying art
Thou choosest the perverse in heart.
To show how rich Thou art Thyself
Thou choosest those that have no wealth.
All glory therefore be to Thee
Who by Thy grace hast chosen me.

Meribah

It's time for us, His sheep, as we
around our shepherds graze
to hearken to The Shepherd's voice,
for each true sheep obeys.
For while the elders rule with grace

and by the book they lead
although true sheep may nip at times,
goats bite the hands that feed.
It's time for judgment to begin
here at the house of God.
The false shall feel damnation's sting,
the true the chastening rod.
If we shall scarce escape the flame,
where shall the man appear
who sits before the Holy Word
but turns away his ear?

Lamentations 3

I am the man who feels Your wrath,
and, smitten with Your holy rod,
my strength has failed, hope's almost gone.
for You have left me, O my God.
Remember my affliction great,
my misery and grievous woe,
the bitterness of my complaint,
for You have brought me very low.
My soul remembers all her pain
and bows herself into the dust.
Yet in my pain You are my hope,
for in no other can I trust.
Because You, Lord, are very kind
our sinful souls are not consumed;
because Your mercies fail us not
we perish not with all the doomed.
Your mercies are renewed each day;
Your faithfulness is very great.
The Lord's my portion, and for Him
my feeble soul will silent wait.
In You I hope; You're good to all

that wait for You and seek Your face.
Therefore I will be hopeful still
and silently will keep my place.
Until You save me from on high
I'll bear the yoke You've placed on me.
I'll sit alone in quietness
because Your hand has humbled me.
I'll put my mouth down in the dust
'til You are pleased to comfort me.
Let him that smites me smite away;
I'll bear it with humility.
My soul is filled full with reproach.
My cheek still feels the smarting blow.
That You will not cast off at last
be pleased to let my spirit know.
You've caused me grief, and yet I see
that in infinity of grace
compassion still is left for me,
and therefore I will seek Your face.
I know it does not please You, Lord,
to smite Your child with stern intent;
and yet, what happens on the earth
but what Your mighty hand has sent?
Why does a living man complain
when You, Lord, smite him for his sin?
Come, let us search and try our ways
and turn back to the Lord again.

Psalm 88

O God of my salvation great
to You I cry both night and day.
Let my prayer come before Your face,
and listen, Lord, to what I say.
My soul is full of troubles dark.

In Sorrow and In Joy

    My life draws near unto the grave.
    I'm counted with those nearly dead,
    like man who has no strength to save.
    The slain lie free within the grave,
    and You remember them no more.
    You've laid me in the lowest pit,
    in darkness and in depths full sore.
    Your wrath lies hard upon my soul;
    You have afflicted me with woe.
    My friends are fled away from me,
    with loathing far away they go.
    I am shut up in prison dark,
    I cannot rise and venture out.
    Mine eyes are mourning in my grief,
    and in my woe to You I shout.
    Will You show wonders to the dead?
    Will they arise and praise Your name?
    Will lovingkindness be recalled,
    or any dead man sing Your fame?
    To You I've cried in my distress.
    The night and morning hear my sighs.
    Why have You cast my soul away,
    and from my spirit hid Your eyes?
    I was distressed and full of woe
    from childhood to this very day.
    Your fierce wrath billows over me;
    Your terrors frighten me always.
    They come upon me like a flood;
    they circle me on every side.
    My loving friends are turned away;
    In darkness You my spirit hide.

White Stone

White stone and whiter name,
a spirit free from blight,
the city fair of purest gold
that knoweth not the night;
a new and endless song,
the healing leaves for all,
the Presence of the Righteous One,
reversal of the Fall;
Sweet, high eternal praise,
Good company and peace,
free worship of the Holy One;
pain, tears, and death all cease.

Dark stone and darker name,
a spirit full of woe,
a city full of filth and pain
where nothing pure doth go;
a sad, imperfect song,
by sickness many fall;
the Righteous One is dimly seen,
the veil cov'reth all;
mixed peace and grievous pain,
our highest joy is gray.
Up! Run, press, pray, and struggle on;
Tomorrow breaketh Day.

Job

Cursed be the day that I was born.
May God not bless it from on high.
Why do You mark my every step,
weigh my sins and make me sigh?
You, Mighty God, contend with me.

In Sorrow and In Joy

I cannot answer You at all—
not one of many charges laid.
Who but deserves damnation's gall?
No man is pure before Your sight,
O Wise in Heart and Full of Strength.
You have chastised me very sore
and stretched my soul to fullest length.
If I were righteous, yet my tongue,
my own mouth would confess my shame.
I know You will not find me pure:
Unblemished, holy is Your name.
My soul is weary of my life.
I will speak freely my complaint.
O God, condemn me not, I pray.
Why should You strive 'til I am faint?
Have You the eyes of mortal men,
or are Your years like one of these?
Because You search out all my sin,
probing my loathsome, foul disease.
Your hands have made me, and they mar.
Remember, I beseech You, Lord,
that You have made me from the clay.
Will You destroy me with a word?
If I be wicked, woe to me;
if I be righteous, I'll not boast.
I am confused, behold my plight.
Against me strives a valiant host.
And You are hunting for my soul
as mighty lions hunt their prey.
You have renewed Your charges, Lord,
and grown more angry every day.
Why came I forth out of the womb?
O that I had not lived one hour!
Are not my days fast fled away?
Then comfort me in grace and power.

The One who stretched the heavens out,
upholding all by wisest might,
Who made the great, ferocious beasts,
as well as ruling day and night;
This One I see with faith's bold eye.
Wherefore myself I do abhor.
I do repent in ash and dust.
Come, gracious Lord, my heart restore.

Isaiah 12

With thanks upon this day of grace
my cheerful soul will pray,
"Though You were angry for my sins,
Your wrath is turned away."
My hot damnation fell on Him
Who died my soul to save.
With Christ Himself and pardoning grace
You also comfort gave.
Behold, my rescue is in God;
I'll trust and never fear.
The Lord Jehovah is my strength;
my song shall reach His ear.
Yes, He is my salvation great,
my well-spring full of grace.
My people, praise the Lord your God,
cry out, and seek His face.
Make mention that His name is high;
sing to the Lord, shout praise.
You must rejoice, for God the Lord
shall dwell with You always.

White Robe

See here this robe of purest white;
one hand did weave it all.
I dare not add one thread to it;
I've none unstained by gall.
It's made with intricate design;
it needs no ornament.
And He that wove it to my soul
this garment did present.
It's made to cover scar and sin,
and guilt and grievous shame.
The One who made it bought it dear,
and Holy is His name.
I wear it now; I'll wear it too
upon the coming Day
in which the elements shall melt,
the heavens pass away.
This is my cov'ring, bright and good,
this is my wedding-dress,
all pure and washed in sacred blood:
Jesus, Your righteousness.

Job (II)

You have smitten all my crop,
made my pleasant leaves to drop,
stricken peace and joy with blight,
turned my comforts into night.
To what profit is my health?
Gnawing rust consumes my wealth.
Yet withal I mercy see;
one great gift You've given me,
sweetest fruit of holy Vine,
Hallelujah! God is mine!

Untitled

Man may chide me or despise
or else may praise with flattery,
but I am humbled, O my God,
by what You know my heart to be.

Grace

I fear Your anger, vengeance, wrath,
dark glances of Your face,
but far more awful than all these
the full-eyed gaze of grace.

Hope

He'll give His angels charge of you,
your foot you shall not dash,
though he that hopes in God 'scapes not
the Father's chastening lash.
He'll have you cast on Him alone;
He'll draw you from the net
When your own arm is not your hope
but all on Him is set.
It's ours hearken to His voice
and cry to Him for grace.
It's His to hear and rescue us
from His high, holy place.

In Sorrow and In Joy

For Joel

(Welcome Home)

From the far country,
sick and defiled,
riches all squandered,
unworthy child!
No longer haughty,
penitent bow.
What does your Father
think of you now?
"Lord, I've done evil"
to Him you say.
"Make me your servant,
Father, I pray."
"No! Bring the best robe,
sandals and ring.
Serve him a banquet
fit for a king."
Heaven rejoices,
Trinity smiles.
Brother, we all came
as many miles.

Meditation

Wicked envy, blindest rage
pursued 'til You were dead.
'Twas not their hate that brought You there;
Your own hands broke the bread.
Fiery wrath of outraged God
against me filled the cup.
But willingly You drank it all
and left me wine to sup.

At The Table

Sin told me it was sweetest bliss.
I found out that it lied.
I know no richer, sweet delight
than Jesus crucified.

Paradox

O Christ, Thou lovest righteousness.
How canst Thou then love me?
Thine eyes are holy, piercing, pure . . .
Dost Thou no evil see?
If man but knew what's in my heart
he surely would condemn.
But Thou, both Priest and Sacrifice,
dost wash me yet again.

Computers and Creation

Blinking lights and wiry miles,
I/O errors, random files,
all man mints is but a slug.
Don't believe it? Pull the plug.
God's intentions rule the stars,
keep the seas behind their bars.
God made all things, I insist.
Men say, "He does not exist."

After Long Illness

Long asleep, now awake,
rust-encrusted pitchfork take.
Tangled harness, cob-webbed plow,
fields dormant wait thee now.
Empty barns, the horses strayed,
heart-work must not be delayed.
Illness sometimes dullness breeds;
fields let lie go straight to weeds.

Drought

Dry as dust,
Rebellion desiccates my trust.
Faith so small,
And scaly as the eyes of Saul.
Cracked by thirst,
O sprinkle me as at the first.
Lord, send rain!
O soften my parched heart again.

Romans 8:26

I find I have no words to say.
Am I Thine own?
My heart doth moan
and cannot utter what I pray.
Dost Thou despise me from Thy Throne?
O draw Thou near, Great God, and hear—
the Comforter for me doth groan.
Yea, Christ for me doth intercede.
It shall be well;
I fear not hell;
With His own blood the Word doth plead.

And Thou Their voice dost ever hear.
Both sin and pain,
though they remain,
can never turn away Thine ear.

Fruitfulness

Like this old apple tree,
twisted and marred,
so is my spirit, Lord,
battered and scarred.
Still though it lift each branch
heav'nward this day,
not one of them doth go
straight on its way.
How doth my spirit twist
backwards from Thee!
Yet still my heart doth yearn
Thy face to see.
O grant the Springtime, Lord,
refreshing shower,
that I may persevere,
strengthened with power,
lest at the Harvest-time
Thy heart should grieve
if Thou should'st find on me
nothing but leaves.

On Election Day

There was but one Election Day
before the world began
when Sovereign Mercy looked in grace
upon the likes of man.

Longing

O wherefore art Thou gone, my Priest,
so long within the veil?
Wilt Thou not ever come out thence,
and mine eyes, waiting, fail?
If Thou yet linger long, my Lord,
O bid me come to Thee!
My steps by faith shall firm and sure
though through the tempest be.
I need not fear the raging wave,
nor wind, nor seething tide,
for he whom Thou dost bid to come
shall safe with Thee abide.

Maranatha

Come, Lord, and roll the heavens up,
descend with Dooms-day shout!
Unlock the iron gates of sin
and let Your people out.
Why will You have half-hearted praise
when You deserve the whole?
For sweeter, purer love shall breathe
from each perfected soul
the day that You conclude the work
and bid Your saints arise.
Come, Lord, no longer let us grope,
but open all our eyes.

On The Feast

Come, Brethren, let us keep the feast
without a trace of leaven.
The next time we rejoice with Him,
(who knows?) may be in heaven.

Confidence

Rock solid as His firm decree,
my Hope and Anchor sure,
Christ stands within the veil for me,
and I need nothing more.

Assurance

For all Thy loving chastisement,
I thank Thee, O my God.
I've learned that Thou my Father art,
for Thy hand held the rod.

For a Lady Who is Ill

O firm support of endless grace,
Sweet coverlet of peace!
His real presence comfort you
and make your pains to cease.
In your affliction, He is near,
His wings about your head.
Yes, God stoops down to care for you;
His own hand makes your bed.

In Sorrow and In Joy

For My Brother
(In Consideration of his Thirty-Third Birthday)

If he should leave them not a dime
they shall have treasure all the same.
With warm reproof and earnest love,
the good man leaves his child his name.

Affliction (II)

Thy saints are ever in the fire;
they suffer shame and pain and loss.
But how else should the truth be known
that they are silver and not dross?

On the Marriage of a Widow With Children

Blessed art Thou, Lord Most High,
Who hast heard the orphan's cry,
mercy to the widow showed,
on the faint Thy grace bestowed;
For their need Thou dost supply.
Blessed art Thou, Lord Most High.

Affliction (III)

All my heart this day rejoices
though I'm in the white-hot flame
for the Son of God is with me.
Blessed be His Holy Name!

In Sorrow and In Joy

On The Death of an Elder

He bowed his head and heart to pray
and, lo, the shadows passed away.
He saw Him Whom he loved unseen,
the veil of flesh no more between.
Death's birth-pang passed so swiftly by,
and endless glory met his eye.

Psalm 116

I love the Lord because He hears
my voice of prayer whene're I cry.
Because my God gives ear to me
I'll call upon Him 'til I die.
The cords of death surrounded me,
and hell's sharp pains my soul distressed.
Instead of joy I sorrow found
and trouble more than peace and rest.
Therefore I cried unto the Lord,
"O God, I pray, deliver me."
The Lord is gracious unto all,
that He is merciful I see.
The Lord preserves the simple man.
I was brought low; then He did save.
Return unto your rest, my soul,
for unto you He mercy gave.
You have preserved my soul from death,
mine eyes from tears lest I should fall.
So will I walk before Your throne,
before Your chosen people all.
I have believed; therefore I speak
although I was in bitter woe
and said that no man speaks the truth,

at least not any that I know.
What shall I render to the Lord
for all His lovingkindness shown?
I'll take salvation's cup with joy
and call this God in prayer my own.
And unto Him I'll pay my vows,
yes, even in His people's sight.
To Him the dying saint is dear,
His people ever His delight.
O Lord, I am Your child indeed,
the son of the free woman, Lord.
Since You have loosed my chafing chain,
sweet praise to You I will accord.
I'll give You thanks before Your saints,
yes, all shall hear my songs of praise
within Your house, Jerusalem,
I'll endless Hallelujahs raise.

Purification

(Leviticus 13:56–58)

I look upon my woven work
and, lo, at once I grieving find
that devious sin doth twist and work
and in the very fabric twine.
Lord, rend Thou out the leprous spot
and in Thy blood wash Thou my soul.
Then shall my heart indeed be clean
and every whit be pure and whole.

Fear

(Revelation 21:8)

Since Thou hast, Lord, against the coward
such awful curses laid,
'tis not my fears that fright me most
but that I am afraid.

On Stony Ground

Thy sun arises blazing hot;
not all plants by it thrive.
I bless Thee, Lord of Harvest high,
that I am yet alive.

Bitterness

Since God Most High has brought me low
and covered me with shame,
no longer Pleasant call thou me,
but Mara is my name.

Sweetness

The thoughts of man at very best
are not like Thy sweet Word to me;
no earthly notion tastes as sweet
as bittersweet Reality.

In Sorrow and In Joy

Habakkuk 3

I know that You will come to judge.
I heard Your voice and was afraid.
O Lord, revive Your work again,
and many years grant us Your aid.
In wrath remember mercy, Lord,
Who soon shall draw in judgment nigh.
Your glory covers earth with praise;
Your radiance fills all the sky.
His brightness as the noonday sun,
and hidden in His hand was power.
Before Him went the pestilence,
and burning coals beneath devour.
He stood and measured all the earth;
He scattered nations with a word.
The everlasting mountains shook,
and all the hills His judgments heard.
His ways are everlasting. He
the heathen nations will affright.
But why was God so angry then,
and why did He the mountains smite?
The mountains saw You and they feared;
the sea's dark depths in terror roared.
The sun and moon stood still for fear
before the glory of the Lord.
In fury did You march abroad,
and crushed the earth in anger just
to save by Your Anointed's hand
the humble poor that in You trust.
You smote the rulers who with pride
against Your own put forth their might.
The poor their soul devoured with glee;
You brought their works before Your sight.
I heard You, and I was afraid,

for I shall their destruction see.
My lips have quivered, and my bones
in rottenness consume away.
For You will surely come to judge,
and what will then become of me
when You shall come as mighty hosts
and all the earth from You shall flee?
The fig tree will not bear her flower,
nor will the vine fruition see.
The olive's work shall be in vain,
and in the fields no fruit shall be.
Yet will my soul rejoice in God,
with joy the God of mercy sing.
He is my strength, and though He smite,
He yet remains my gracious King.
My feet shall walk upon the hills,
high places sweet of rest and peace.
Let all His people praise His grace
Who made His wrath toward us to cease.

On The Opening of a New Place of Worship

If Thou go not with us, dear Lord,
then carry us not hence.
O dwell with us, Thy living stones,
Our Rock and Our Defense.
O purify Thy people, Lord,
our expectation raise.
Without the signs that men can see
receive our prayers and praise.
Then truly as in days of old
if Thou draw near in grace
although no eye shall see Thee near,
the cloud shall fill the place.

In Doubting Castle

He lay in Doubt's cold fortress high,
and Old Despair paid him a call.
He thought to win because he sighed,
but Grace would not let Christian fall.
Though giants gave knife, poison, rope,
the key of promise was his hope.

The Thanksgiving

I thank You, O my gracious God,
for house and lands and such,
though as I am a pilgrim here,
I cannot carry much.

Psalm 141

O Lord, I lift my voice to Thee;
make haste to me and hear my cries.
Let my prayer be as sacrifice,
my lifted hands as incense rise.
Set watchmen, Lord, to guard my tongue;
O keep my lips lest I should sin.
Incline my heart to righteous ways
lest there be wickedness within.
Let godly men my soul reprove;
it shall be precious oil refined,
blows from an honest, righteous heart
like sweet perfume, a gift most kind.
And I shall bless them in their woe.
In judgment who shall yet remain?
Thy good Word only will I hear,
forever Scripture my refrain.

Our bones are strewn around our graves
as if we had no greater worth
than wood which cutters cleave in two
and leave it scattered on the earth.
But mine eyes look to Thee, my God.
In Thee I trust, Who art mine own.
Cast not my soul in trouble off,
nor leave me, gracious God, alone.
Keep me from their deceptive wiles,
their snares which they have laid in spite.
Though wicked men be cast to hell
O save Thy servant in Thy might.

Humility

It is a wonder passing great,
more high than man can know
that Thou Who Highest art by right
didst also stoop most low.

Hebrews 6:19

The strong man does not hide himself,
the brave man does not flee,
but I have fled for refuge, Lord,
to hide myself in Thee.
With both my hands I grasp the hope,
by grace will not let go;
because my God can never lie
I consolation know.

The Whisper

Lord, suffer not Thy child to slip;
instead, uphold my heart in woe.
I hear the deep voice of Despair;
it is the whisper of the foe.

Aleph

How blessed is the righteous man
who serves You, Lord, with fear,
who keeps Your Word with all his heart,
to You inclines his ear.
By grace his heart is kept from sin,
he walks upon the way
because his heart Your precepts hears,
commanding to obey.
O that my ways were ordered all
to keep Your statutes, Lord.
Then shall I not be put to shame
when I respect Your Word.
I'll praise You with a righteous heart
when I have learned Your law.
I will obey! O leave me not,
O God, my Fear and Awe.

Psalm 142

I cried unto the Lord my God;
to Him I supplication made.
I poured out my complaint to Him
and showed Him why I am afraid.
My spirit could no longer stand.
He knew my dark and bitter path

and saw that they had spread their snares
to catch my soul in vicious wrath.
I looked about on every side;
I found no man to give me aid.
I found no place where I could hide.
They all passed by, nor any stayed.
Therefore I cried unto the Lord.
I said, "In You alone I hide.
You only are my heritage,
and I have nothing else beside.
Attend unto my cry, O God,
for I am humbled very low.
Deliver me from this cold cell,
from them whose cruel spite I know.
O bring my soul from prison out
that I may praise You and rejoice.
The righteous all shall gather round;
we'll praise Your grace with cheerful voice."

Beth

How shall the young man cleanse his way
that he may walk in godly fear?
Let him attend to all Your Word
and to You turn a listening ear.
With my whole heart I sought You, Lord,
From Your commandments I would stray
unless You, Lord, did keep me in
and grant me that I might obey.
Your Word I treasure in my heart
that I against You might not sin.
You only are the Blessed God;
teach me Your holy way within.
How often have my lips declared
Your judgments, righteous, rich, and free.

In Sorrow and In Joy

I have rejoiced in all Your truth,
more precious than fine gold to me.
I will consider all Your Word
and have respect unto Your ways.
I will delight in statutes pure
and cherish Scripture all my days.

Petition

I make but one request:
I pray Thee grant my plea.
I ask not for Thy gifts,
but rather, Lord, for Thee.

On Sincerity

O God have mercy on my soul
lest all my fear be but in word,
lest I draw near but with my mouth
as if Thy voice I had not heard,
lest while my heart is far away
I should Thee honor with my tongue.
Praise shall not as sweet incense rise
if with my heart I have not sung.

Perseverance

Scarcely can I hold secure
to the Rock of Refuge sure.
Yet 'tis not the Rock I see
that is false and slippery.
That my grip may firmer be
take away the slime in me.

In Sorrow and In Joy

Scarcely can I hold secure
to the Rock of Refuge sure.
Though I slip the while I hold
Him Who for my sins was sold,
this shall all my comfort be
that the Rock is holding me.

On The Rebuke

Dear brother, see your honest words,
a plain rebuke from Scripture clear,
far from estranging you from me
have made you rather far more dear.
More than a flowery tongue or pen
a faithful wound a friend must prove
and he that cares the most for me
is he that speaks the truth in love.
I will not hear in word alone;
God has to me this chiding sent.
I will not kick against the goads;
See, faithful brother, I repent.

Psalm 6

My God, rebuke me not, I pray,
and in Your wrath chastise me not,
for fiercely burns Your anger, Lord,
and Your displeasure's deep and hot.
Have mercy, Lord, upon my soul,
for I am weak and sick and low.
My soul is very deeply pained.
How long shall I Your anger know?
Return, O Lord, deliver me.
O save my soul in mercy great.
For in the grave, who ponders You

and at Your courts with thanks will wait?
O! I am weary with my groans,
and through the night I weep and sigh.
My bed is dampened with my tears
and blasting grief consumes mine eye.
Mine eyes are dim because of those
that hate my soul. Let them depart
for God has heard my wordless cries,
the deepest groanings of my heart.
The Lord has heard my earnest pleas,
requests which I have made before.
Let all my foes be put to shame,
and let them trouble me no more.

Again

O! must I come today
as yesterday,
smeared with besetting sin,
slow to obey?
Halting my wounded soul,
bruised though unseen.
Yet will I boldly come,
wash and be clean.
When shall the morning dawn
that I shall stand
with garments always white
and stainless hand?
Though earth know not that peace,
cannot be still,
and rest will never know,
yet heaven will.

Thanksgiving

I cannot hold my peace, dear Lord,
nor can I curb my tongue
until I've blessed Your matchless name
and joyful praises sung.
Who is like You among the gods?
I would be in my grave
if vanities had been my help
which have no strength to save.
You had commanded by Your Word,
I trembled to obey
but Mercy would not let me rest
but drove me in Your way.
You do not always rescue me
when first I cry for aid
For I must learn to keep Your law
even when I am afraid.
You rescued me and heard my cry
upon this blessed day.
Now in Your faithful, tender love
grant more grace to obey.

On a Word Shot From a Distance

Lord, You have drawn Your mighty bow
and from it shot a single dart
which hit me where it hurt the most,
right in my swollen, festering heart.
O do not let me break the shaft
nor leave my mattering heart alone
'til from it, pressed out, washed in blood,
each putrid drop of pus is gone.

Humility (II)

Lord, grant me meek humility
with Your sweet graces all,
for he that bends him very low
has not so far to fall.

Fall

When conscience cries aloud
and I will not give ear
but stuff a rotten rag
into its mouth, or fear
the face of mortal man
more than my God withal,
as when dry leaves blow 'round
they are the signs of Fall.

Winter

By this cold, wint'ry blast
in which You hide Your face
nor warm my soul at all
with tender, fond embrace,
O grant my chilly heart
what more than peace it needs:
O freeze my vermin, Lord,
and also all my weeds.

Spring

When Thou dost first begin
to show Thy blessed face
and warm my chilly soul

with tender, fond embrace,
then mercy doth appear
like flowers in the snow.
If Thou didst plant them not,
who did? I do not know.

Summer

When with a conscience clear
and with submission sweet
I in Thy bosom lie
or kiss Thy blessed feet
then like a summer day
by no harsh wind distressed
my weary soul at peace
may ever calmly rest.

Micah 7

Ah! Woe is me, for I am spent
as when the summer fruits are gone;
each cluster gathered from the vine,
my soul finds not a single one.
The godly man is perished quite;
no upright man remains as yet,
for each man lies in wait for blood
to catch his brother in the net.
For evil they pursue with haste.
The prince and judge seek their rewards;
the great man seeks perverse desires
and no man honesty regards.
The best of them is as a briar
and sharpened as a cruel thorn.
Their day of visitation comes,
and wrath shall rise with breaking morn.

In Sorrow and In Joy

    Beware and do not trust your friend,
    nor confidence put in a guide,
    and even from your wedded wife
    you must your words both guard and hide;
    for son dishonors father now,
    and daughter rises up in hate.
    A man's own brethren are his foes
    and those that lie for him in wait.
    But I will look unto the Lord
    and wait for God to rescue me;
    my God will hear my bitter cry
    and save me from mine enemy.
    Yea, though I fall, I shall arise,
    and though I sit in deepest night
    the Lord arising in His grace
    shall be my everlasting light.
    And though I bear His bitter wrath
    (for I have sinned against my Lord)
    my God will yet my cause maintain,
    and in His justice will reward
    my foes and bring me forth to light.
    Mine eyes His righteousness shall see.
    Then shall my foe be put to shame
    who said in hatred unto me,
    "Where is your God?" When judgment falls
    you and all men shall surely know.
    For judgment comes with certainty
    and all defenses crumble low.
    For He shall come, the Mighty Lord,
    dear Shepherd of His chosen few,
    Who feeds His people with His rod,
    Whose mercies are forever new.
    The nations then shall be amazed;
    astonished shall they silent be,
    for they shall tremble at Thy might,

and all shall be afraid of Thee.
For who is like the Living God
Who sin forgives and passes by
the wickedness of all His own
though for their sins they ought to die?
The Lord does not retain His wrath
for mercy is His great delight,
and of Himself His anger stills
and all our sins has put to right.
Yes, He has cast them in the depths;
There have our sins their wat'ry grave,
for He will keep His promised oath
Who swore in mercy us to save.

Balaam

I need not fear that man will smite
and cause my soul distress.
No man that lives and breathes can curse
if Thou command to bless.

Refuge

O'ershade me with Thy feathers, Lord,
and hide me 'neath Thy wing.
Then shall I sweetly nestle safe
beside my Mighty King.
That fierce affliction is my friend
that drives me to draw near.
For Thou wast ever present, Lord,
more in the cloud than clear.

Perspective (II)

If I at length shall persevere,
all glory to the King!
For in myself I know full well
there dwelleth no good thing.

Gimel

O bless Thy servant, gracious Lord,
that I may live and keep Thy Word,
and open Thou mine eyes to see
Thy glory in the Scriptures, Lord.
I am a stranger in the earth.
Hide not Thy righteous law from me.
My soul is longing for Thy Word,
Thy judgments precious as can be.
Thou hast rebuked the proud in heart,
the cursed ones that go astray.
Remove from me reproach and shame
because Thy precepts I obey.
Though mighty men against me speak,
Thy servant thinks upon Thy will.
Thy testimonies make me glad
and they shall be my teachers still.

He

Teach me Thy statutes, gracious Lord,
and I will keep them to the end.
Give me to understand Thy law,
for to obey Thee I intend.
O make me walk where Thine own law

doth lead; for it is my delight.
And turn my heart to righteous ways
and not to things of sense and sight.
O turn mine eyes from vanity
and quicken me upon the way.
Lord, prove Thy Word unto my soul;
Thy servant feareth Thee this day.
O turn away my dark reproach,
the shame which every day I fear.
Thy judgments, Lord, are very good;
I long Thy precepts pure to hear.
Behold, my Lord, and give me life
in greater measures on the way
that in Thy strength and fear my soul
may all Thy righteous Word obey.

Job (III)

Why do You strive with me each day
and smite me with Your mighty rod?
I would complain against Your ways,
but I am man and You are God.

For Graduation from a Faithful Seminary

Lord, make them godly men
of humble, reverent fear
that see Thee, Everlasting King,
and to Thee bend their ear.
Lord, make them holy men
that keep Thy Word with awe.
O that within their heart might burn
the fire of Thy law!
Lord, make them faithful men

of conscience clean and pure.
May they delight Thee to obey
that all their steps be sure.
Lord, make them joyful men
that Thee unseen behold;
O warm their heart with mercy sweet
lest ev'n their love grow cold.
Lord, make them prayerful men,
their weapons sharp and bright,
and draw Thou near with needed aid
when fierce shall grow the fight.
Lord, thrust Thy servants out
into Thy harvest field
that through their toil Thou mayest see
of Thy deep woe the yield.
O grant that that sweet day
on which our labour ends
may find them all through mercy great
not as Thy foes but friends.

Magdalene

Since You have brought me very low
yet do I think it sweet
that though my heart is filled with woe
You let me kiss Your feet.
And with the tears Your pains provoke
which on Your feet I shed,
forgiving, washing all away,
You will perfume my head.

In Sorrow and In Joy

Obedience (For Bear)

I bid my puppy sit and stay,
and he at once must run away;
or if to go shall be my law
he will not stir a single paw.
He neither listens to my voice
nor makes my will his happy choice.
And shall I give, my Lord, to Thee
dishonor, as my dog gives me?
For when Thou bid'st me wait Thy will
I fret and whine and whimper still.
That I may honor Thy great Name,
I pray Thee, Lord, Thy Rover tame.

Enlightenment

Since You are come to heal my soul
then I will think it grace
if You should take me by the hand
or spit into my face.
And though my sight be dim and blurred
yet I shall see aright
the things by faith I handle now
if You but give me light.

On Princeton Chapel

Awake, awake, you ancient wood,
and you archaic stones,
for what you have not felt for years
shall stir in your old bones.
You vaulted arches richly carved,
so darkly draped with night,

your elder eyes this day shall see
the everlasting light.
Now hear the Scriptures once again.
Come, you old walls, rejoice!
This day your waiting ears shall hear
a gospel Preacher's voice.

Affliction (IV)

My gracious God, I give You thanks
that though You give me lands and wealth
my grieving soul cannot rejoice
if You should but withhold Yourself.

Mark 5:28

See, from behind Thee in the press
where Thou art gone Thine own to bless
I secretly drew near to Thee
to seek for mine infirmity
to touch Thy garment, Lord.
O! With Thy mighty power and Word
My fountain of iniquity
which from my heart doth endlessly
defilement spew forth in me
I pray Thee stop and seal.
Turn, Gracious Lord, and heal my soul;
let that same mercy make me whole
that moved Thee first to pass this way
and that sweet Providence display
which drew me unawares.

Manasseh

Blest was Manasseh's iron chain
above his golden crown,
for this did lift him up in pride
while that did cast him down.
And blessed was his prison-house
above his throne so high,
for when he sought God from the depths
He heard his bitter cry.
O blessed fierce affliction sharp!
O blessed grievous pain!
For with these in mine iron heart
Thou dost draw near again.

Shame

Bold Shame! for what cause do you rise
and spread your naught before mine eyes?
You think to make me quit the field
by that Reproach you whet and wield;
you whisper Scandal in mine ear
but I will conquer you with Fear.

On Nearly Nine Years in the Pew

I sit before Thy mighty Word,
a sea of glory vast,
and like a dry sponge into it
my thirsty soul is cast.
What a rich feast of meat and wine
before mine eyes is spread!
Here ravenous, I take my fill
of this sweet Living Bread.

Chastisement (II)

With fierce affliction Thou dost smite
and chasten my heart so,
but I must ask where I might be
if Thou didst let me go.

Grace (II)

Who am I, Lord, and who are mine
that You should kindly look toward me?
Bless'd be discriminating grace
and mercy's sweet infinity.

To My Shepherds

Pastors dear,
How kind Our Lord,
(Chiefest Shepherd of His flock),
is in giving you to us
that when hiding in the Rock
finding in our wool a burr
you may kindly it remove,
and if you must wield the rod
never touch it but in love.
How blest is this sorry sheep!
In Christ's fold I sweetly feed,
taught by honest shepherds true
that my Lord is all I need.
Please accept this little note
which is written gratefully.
Let me tell you this once more
that I love you
                Sheepishly

Submission

As Thou wilt, Almighty God,
be it after Thy decree.
Thou art good and doest good,
faithfully afflicting me.

Mordecai's Song

Ah, poor Ahasueras!
You will not sleep the night
that He who reigns in heaven and earth
begins to set things right.

Resistance

Think, my soul, if sin entice
thee to think thou cans't afford
one indulgence (O so small!),
what price hath it cost thy Lord?

Confession (II)

Since my heart Thou knowest, Lord,
and that sin its springs dost touch,
I could scarcely think I erred
if I owned it overmuch.

Rest

When Your Covenant You press,
arguing Your faithfulness,
crediting one Offering,
real forgiveness promising,
Smitten conscience finds its rest
quiet on the Saviour's breast.

Chastisement (III)

Perhaps because my heart was hard
by practice, birth, and will,
You chose to use Your iron rod
my waywardness to kill.
I know not why, my gracious Lord,
You've brought me grief and pain,
but knowing this road leads to You,
I on it still remain.

From Job 36

From the righteous man, O Lord,
Thou dost not withdraw Thine eye,
but with kings thou sett'st him up
and his heart dost satisfy.
If in fetters he be bound,
in affliction trapped and tied,
then Thou showest him his work
and that he hath walked in pride.
Opening his inner ear
Thou to teach him dost begin
and command him by Thy law
that he should return from sin.

If he listen and obey
in prosperity shall he
pass his swiftly fleeting days,
and in pleasures shall he be.
But if he should hearken not,
he shall perish by the sword;
he shall die in ignorance,
meriting the anger stored;
godless, treasuring up wrath,
crying not if Thou afflict,
he shall die with the perverse,
cursed beneath Thine interdict.
The afflicted by their woe
Thou deliverest, O Lord,
out of their compressing strait
when Thou hast their soul allured.

Healing

(Job 34:31–32)

Lord, I have borne chastisement.
I will not offend Thee more.
What I see not, teach Thou me,
on my wounds Thy mercy pour.

Fear (II)

Jesus, Mighty Shepherd kind,
ministering to the mind,
Thou dost bid Thy little flock
nestling within the Rock,
to recall Thy Father's will
gracious purpose to fulfill
royal place to them to give

(for they shall forever live)
and, their fainting heart to cheer
by Thy love, to cast out fear.

To My Physician

If one's arm should be gangrenous,
what straightway will he do?
His limb he stretches to the knife
and pays the surgeon too.
But I have got a cancer.
In my heart it inheres.
And, Lord, unless You cut it out
it will fulfill my fears.
It is a putrid sight, Lord,
which I know that You see;
mere bandages and medicines
will not suffice for me.
Affliction is the scalpel
with which You're healing me.
I weep but for the moment,
then praise will be Your fee.

On His Manhood

Who is this Who leads the song
of the gathered holy throng?
Who is this exalted high,
reigning throned in majesty?
Who is this, a virgin's child,
holy, harmless, undefiled?
Who is this Who gave His bride
His own blood and gifts beside?
Who is this that sorrow knew?

Pain, frustration, anger too?
Who is this that trembled still,
facing God His Father's will?
Seed of Abraham is He,
yet incarnate Deity.
This is He Who knows our frame,
bore our guilt and all our shame.
Why does He, the glorious King
prayer to His father bring?
He remembers all our woe
Who this earthly way did go.
This is He in Whom we trust,
made like us of earth and dust.
This is He, Christ Jesus, Lord.
Let Him be by all adored.

Communion Meditation

Could He not pity from afar
whose hand has formed the evening star?
Why did He stoop from yonder throne
to make a crown of thorns His own?
For nothing could more righteous be
than that He damn the likes of me,
and yet, in mercy great and high
God becomes man that He may die.
The Christ must work and sweat and bleed
that He might captives captive lead.
My soul, for thee He tasted hell;
see that thou therefore love Him well.

Expectation

Come, thou Resurrection Day!
Come, Eternal Sabbath, stay!
When the church, His holy bride
shall be gathered to His side.
When our hands shall touch and feel
what by faith we know is real.
Gather all Thy children home!
Come, Lord Jesus, quickly come.

Incarnation

Man made high and God made low;
who this mystery can know?
He in swaddling clothes was found;
with my grave cloths was He wound.
God doth bleed while man doth cry;
dead men live, for Life doth die.
Since my thorns He made His own
I shall share His very throne.

Psalm 121

In my distress I lift mine eyes
unto the mountains high.
From whence shall my Redeemer come
Who shall my need supply?
My help is from the Living God
Who made both dark and light.
He only has the strength to save
the wisdom and the might.
He will not let your footsteps slip;
on watch He does not sleep.
His constant vigil Israel's God

in faithfulness will keep.
The Lord will keep you. He your great
Protector sure will be.
Nor sun by day nor moon by night
shall smite you vengefully.

Psalm 43

Judge me, O God, and plead my cause
against a wicked land.
Deliver me from lying tongues
and from the unjust man.
You are my God, my only strength.
Why cast my soul away?
Why do I mourn while enemies
oppress me every day?
Send out Your light and truth for me
and let them guide my way.
O bring me to Your holy hill
and endless Sabbath day!
Then will I come before my God,
my joy and great delight,
and praise Him with stringed instruments
and music sweet and light.
My soul, why are you grieving still;
why restless and afraid?
Hope in your God. I yet shall praise
My Help and timely Aid.

On His Fetters

Hush, my soul, do not complain
though God bring you grief and pain,
though in bonds you long have lain.
Maybe this was Joseph's chain.

In the iron I will creep;
from within it will I weep.
And when I have learned to trust,
I shall find this chain but rust.

On the Church Gathering for Worship

Quiet is the holy place
but the rising sun
beams with a refreshing grace:
Sabbath has begun.
Quickly, softly, rank on rank
lines each living stone.
Hurry, for the King is near,
coming to His own.
Range each large and little stone,
then set up the gates.
Even now to enter in
Heaven's Monarch waits.
Sweet the smell of rising prayer,
hearty living bread.
Meat and milk and water too,
new life for the dead.
Slowly sinking setting sun,
mournful evensong.
Come, eternal Sabbath day!
Blessed Lord, How long?

Extra Verses for Psalm 42 as Set in the Trinity Hymnal

My tears have been my daily food;
continually they say,
"Where is thy God? Why doth He not

come to thine aid today?"
When I remember all these things,
my soul's poured out abroad.
For I had gone with joy to praise
Thee in Thy house, O God.

Invocation

Come, Lord, all Thy temple fill;
animate each living stone.
Take the worship and the praise
that is due to Thee alone.
None shall share Thy rightful place;
every knee shall bow.
Let the offering be pure
that we bring Thee now.

Hardening

Sweet conscience, like a silver lake,
must be kept clear, for conscience' sake.
Else, as in winter, by degrees
that which was soft begins to freeze,
and that which could not bear a pin
now bears a cartload full of sin.
I need Thy light to warm my soul
lest winter's blast my heart control.
I feel this sharp and icy frost;
Lord, help me now, or all is lost.

Baptism

Into the water our Jesus went
by God the Father for sinners sent.
Thirsty our sinful spirits to bless,
He came fulfilling all righteousness.
He all our burdens did undertake,
propitiation for us to make,
His Holy Father to glorify,
Jesus came forth to suffer and die.
Into the water I come today
I His command in Scripture obey.
No hope have I but in Jesus' blood
in my heart finding nothing that's good.
Christ, my Redeemer, You there for me
did bind Yourself to set my soul free.
Therefore in water I faith profess
You are my Saviour; You I confess.

Baptism (II)

Once in water, once in anger
You were baptized, Lord, for me;
fiery billows of God's ire
You endured most willingly.
On Your name I called believing,
washing all my sins away;
and my conscience boldly answers
Jesus is my Hope this day.
I will be Your true disciple.
Lead me, Saviour, by Your Word.
Dying to the world, I leave it,
living unto You, my Lord.
You are all my hope of heaven,

In Sorrow and In Joy

You my righteousness shall be.
In this water I confess You
as my Saviour public'ly.

On Aging

I have been young; now I am old, but never did I see
a godly man in dire straights forsaken utterly.
While brown, then grey, then silver hairs adorned my aging head,
I never saw a good man's children begging for their bread.

At Interpreter's House

See how the water sputters the flame!
And yet in secret, loving His name,
that all this fire I should not lose,
here stands One pouring oil from His cruise.
Buckets and buckets fiendish foes pour
(I think this happened sometime before)
secret grace flowing fresh from His hand,
fire burns water at His command.

At Interpreter's House (II)

Sir, set down my name, said he,
who would fight most valiantly.
Many wounds he gave and got.
Was it worth it? Who thinks not?
Little while he fought with sin;
said the Blessed "Enter in."

Forgiveness

Business we have to do, for much I owe.
Lord, I will nothing pay; please let me go.
When I my debtor meet, grant me to take
and shred his payment-book, for Thy love's sake.
Thus, by Thy bitter cry, sweeten my gall,
and in Thy flowing blood, cleanse my sins all.
Lord, with Thy broken flesh, mend my soul's breach
as with these elements Thy death I preach.
O, in my darkness, Lord, show me Thy light.
Dripping with precious blood shall I be white.
Then, as I face my Judge, "Guilty" my plea,
"Righteous" His verdict is: One died for thee.

Longing (II)

Whenever I this puppy leave
his little heart begins to grieve,
and not content with ball or bone
at once this pup begins to moan.
He knows that I cannot despise
his howls and yelps and piteous cries.
So, Lord my God, hear Thou my voice,
with Thy return make me rejoice.

On the Mystery of Providence

How great Thou art, God only wise,
who hidest Thy work from mortal eyes,
who from the vilest, filthy sin
though it be evil from within
without defilement Thou dost take
and from it purest good dost make.
If Thou didst use the good and fair

man might perhaps with Thee compare
but providence adverse and strange
Thou, Lord, dost shape and rearrange.
Where sin has had its worst effect
Thou gaping death dost resurrect.

Psalm 4

Answer when I call, O God, my righteousness.
You have set me free when I was in distress.
Lord, have mercy on me; listen to my cry.
How long will this people my soul villify?
How long will the wicked cherish vanity?
How long in oppression will his pleasure be?
But the Lord the godly for Himself reserves;
God my Saviour listens, Who my soul preserves.
Hush, my soul, in anger do not wicked be.
Meditate at evening, silent, privately.
In your anger sin not; let your heart be still.
Offer righteous offerings, trust His gracious will.
Many people wonder who will favor show.
Lord, Your gracious presence on us all bestow.
My heart have You gladdened more than theirs at ease.
Safely will I lie down; my God gives me peace.

If Thou Canst

In this dark, dry wilderness
my soul finds no relief,
but if Thou canst do anything
help Thou mine unbelief.

On Her Darkness

Dear friend, we have been here before
down the dark stairs and through this door.
Where blinded we for comfort grope,
His oath alone our only hope.
Who hopes what he can clearly see?
God swears things are that yet shall be.
Sees diadems in thorny crowns,
so Faith may swim though Reason drowns.

On Death and Dying

My God, have mercy on my frame
which goes to dust from whence it came;
though dissolution be complete
O make my resurrection sweet.

Burnt at the Stake

Thou dost hold me o'er this flame;
turn me over once again;
baste my spirit with my tears;
smoke me slowly with my fears.
In this tongue-lit flame how long
wilt Thou roast me on and on?
One more turn, another one
'til Thou say to me "Well done."

On a Glass of Wine in the Evening

Give strong drink to the sad of heart;
for mourners let them new wine make,
but He who for our sins would bleed
would not the soporific take.

In Sorrow and In Joy

Trust

Why is it I so hard must try
to trust in Him Who cannot lie,
and why so easy, I inquire,
to trust the quintessential liar?

Eliezer

My heart is broken, well Thou dost know.
Promises spoken so long ago
dust covered lying, yet Thou dost say
that Thou wilt keep them, maybe today.
What wilt Thou give me, now as my share
while this old Damascene stands as mine heir?

Ebenezer

How can I see Thy heart, my God,
when I feel nothing but Thy rod?
While Thy hand crushes me again
Thou swearest Thou hast love to men.
In Thy fierce anger well-deserved,
Thou shak'st me till I am unnerved.
and mocking daily my distress
Thou feedest me my bitterness.
Though blinded by my tears I will
shriek out and howl Thy praises still.
From dark distress to Thee I cry,
Lord, come and save me, else I die.

From Deuteronomy

If through the wilderness Thou lead
to prove and humble me
grant me as Caleb long ago
to wholly follow Thee.
Thou from my prison brought me out
but now through barren lands
I stagger 'neath the blinding sun
o'er burning desert sands.
Hard by the tent of meeting pitched,
grant that I may not stray
until at last the cloud shall rise
and lead me on my way.
Lord, give me angels' food to eat,
from Thy Rock water me,
until the River's flood is passed
and Canaan's shore I see.

For a Ruling Elder

To him who in the house of God
in faithfulness rules well,
to him a double portion yield,
a double honor tell.
And when our Shepherd shall appear
in splendor bye and bye,
a crown of glory shall he have
and that eternally.

In Sorrow and In Joy

Nabal

Since you have come to torment me
without, I think, the right,
I'll tell you nothing, less or more
until the morning light.

For Pastor On His 50th Birthday

(From I Timothy 4)

Unto yourself take careful heed
and to your doctrine faithfully;
so shall you save yourself at last
And those that hear you eagerly.
Your precious gift see you upstir
bestowed by hands of presbyt'ry.
To reading give attention, and
in doctrine show no laxity.
Be nourished in the faithful Word,
and trust the saving God who lives.
For he shall have a real success
who to the truth attention gives.
A faithful Pastor, Christ's own gift,
you are, and though you old may grow,
We'll seek to imitate your faith
And with you, then, to heaven go.

To My Manager

(Genesis 50:20; Romans 8:28)

I know you meant to harm me,
but God is in control,
Who took your ill intention
and made it serve His goal.

In Sorrow and In Joy

For all things work together,
No matter what your aim
To benefit His people
And glorify His Name.

To Pastor, in His Illness

Above all things I wish, dear heart,
that you may be in health
and prosper as your spirit does
with true and lasting wealth.

To the Watkins Family (With Thanks)

'Tis well that you lodge strangers
and cheer them with your prayers
for those of old did sometimes
lodge angels unawares.

                    January 2008

Restoration

Of Job's longsuffering you have heard,
how after losing all
our God restored him once again
his things, both great and small.
And seven sons and daughters fair
were born to him once more.
He gave him doubly what he lost
full measure, running o'er.
Perhaps the day will come for me
when my distress is through.
I'll name the daughter I don't have
Miss Keren Happuch too.

In Sorrow and In Joy

On the Death of Lady, a Standard Poodle

Sweet Lady, gentle flower!
Death brushed by me today
and seized you where you slept
and carried you away.
I would it had been I
and you had lived in peace.
But suffering is over
and you have found release.
What made my father sin
in Eden long ago
to cause you this distress,
this misery and woe?
Perhaps you will be here
When earth is made anew.
No longer any curse
And then-immortal you.

      May, 2008

Michal

As Michal had no child at all
Until the day she died.
So none have I, in Providence,
And I alone abide.
Though children are a gracious gift
Reward of grace no doubt,
Yet some are left in solitude
Posterity without.

Thanks (II)

He who with helpless orphans
Or with the widow shares
Thus images his Maker
Who also counts their hairs.
The loan he gives the Highest
To ease the poor's distress
Will be repaid completely
And his own soul will bless.

With Thanks

To help the orphan in distress
Or widow selflessly,
Before our God religion pure,
Unblemished proves to be.
It speaks a heart conforming to
His heart who reigns above,
Whose kindnesses are infinite
And matchless as His love.
The gift was needed, it is true,
But more than that, the deed
A priceless treasure intimates,
A love to those in need.

Widow's Mite

She cast away the last she had,
One, then the other mite.
I wonder . . . Was she hungering,
though full of joy, that night?

In Sorrow and In Joy

On Losing My House to Foreclosure

"The creditors have come," said she,
"to take my sons away."
Oh who would help her in distress
and all her fears allay?

"Go borrow lots and lots of jars
the Lord commands this day."
the prophet bade her through her tears
his spoken word obey.

"Now take the jars and close the door
and pour out oil" he bade.
And not until they all were full
the flow of oil stayed.

Unless her soul had come to grief
she would not with surprise
have seen Creation taking place
before her very eyes.

Though I have lost my house and land
I will not mourn this day.
I might not see a miracle
In any other way.

Words

I'll say this only once, I hope,
And then I will be gone.
I cannot pun upon the phrase
"*hapax legomenon.*"

In Sorrow and In Joy

Jonah

How sad about poor Jonah!
It is a story grim.
He cared less for the Ninevites
than pagans cared for him.

Dismay

My dogs once liked my cooking,
but then one sorry dawn
I sadly learned they much preferred
dead rodent on the lawn.

Puppies

Growl, growl, hiss and howl,
Snip and snap and yip and yowl.
Chew and shred and munch and rip.
Scamper, tussle, dash, and trip.
Puppies are a lot of fun.
Ask me, I've got more than one.

On Bunhill Fields

Where sleep His own, the Shepherd knows.
through scorching drought and winter snows,
the bustling city passing by,
and yet unseen by mortal eye,
the angels guard the sleeping sheep
'til their last vigil they shall keep
The dead shall rise and live once more,
their suffering forever o'er.

Penitence

O Lord, I cannot lift mine eye
To Thine abode on high.
My sins like Everest rise up
And reach unto the sky.
So I will beat upon my breast
And unto Thee will cry,
"O God, be merciful to me
Or else, alas, I die."
My only hope is in His life
And cruel death in my stead.
His righteousness shall cover me,
His grace lift up my head.
Then shall I come before Thy throne
Upon the judgment day
With confidence and joyful song—
My sins He bore away.

At the Table (II)

When Thou dost come unto Thine own
while they remember Thee
in penitence they humbly cry,
"Be merciful to me."
He sees the weakest knee that bows,
He hears the feeblest voice
that cries "Long Live the King of Kings."
It makes His heart rejoice.

In Sorrow and In Joy

On the Baptism of Carl Vos Watkins

Upon thy brow, dear child, is placed
the covenantal sign.
Thy father's God, thy mother's faith,
be they forever thine.

Thy parents vow before the Lord
to train and nurture thee.
The church assents and promises
their willing aid to be.

God grant the day may come at last
when we our Lord shall bless
to hear thy lips before the church
our holy faith profess.

And then at length when life is done
may we with one accord
rejoice to see thee join with us
in Heaven before our Lord.

We Have a Great High Priest

In all things tempted like as we
That He our Great High Priest might be,
Both very God and fully man
According to the Godhead's plan,
That He His Father might obey
In every right and holy way,
Our righteousness to stablish fast:
First Adam vile, but pure the Last.
Our mortal pain to know and feel
That when His saints before Him kneel,
His grace might cheer them in their strife,

In Sorrow and In Joy

Then grant to them eternal life;
With our pains touched Who our sins bore
That we might live forevermore.

On Dental Work and Silence

I do not like my dentist much.
He makes me "open wide"
So he can drill or scrape or fill
or poke around inside.
And then sometimes to my distress
he deigns to stitch or cut.
I really think I'd safer be
to keep my big mouth shut.

On the Death of a Deacon

I am jealous of you, brother,
that so softly slipped away
while the evening was advancing,
while the church was met to pray.
You have gone to see the Glory
in the land of endless day,
and the people I will cry for
are the ones who have to stay.

For Irena Sandler

I never met you, lady, but I kneel before your grave.
Your courage was majestic as the lives you dared to save.
You suffered for their rescue when at last your work was known,
But the children will remember that you loved them as your own.
The great ones did not notice and did not acknowledge you,
But I offer you my tribute, pray God's blessing on you too.
Let the whole wide world remember what the evil was before,
And let generations future suffer Holocaust no more.

In Sorrow and In Joy

Jesus Wept

Although You are the Lord of Life,
Death's Conqueror, our King,
When standing by Your dear friend's tomb,
You did not laugh or sing.
How tragic was the dreadful day
When Adam disobeyed!
How stark the death his sin incurred,
God's mighty wrath displayed!
You wept beside his grave although
You knew that he would rise,
At once at Your commanding voice,
Again when cleave the skies.
I may lie down, I know not when,
But I am hid in You.
If I should sleep before You come,
I know You'll raise me too.

May, 2010

On the Death of Ed Minor

He came to church this Sunday
though yesterday he died.
His spirit now perfected,
his Lord he sat beside.

No longer seeing darkly
but face to Blessed Face.
No longer shadows only,
but feeling Love's embrace.

No more to sin or sorrow,
no more to fear or sigh,

In Sorrow and In Joy

his Father's hand removing
the last tear from his eye.

With his perfected brethren
the saints that went before
to gaze upon the Glory,
to worship and adore.

How blest not just their mem'ry
but these, the sainted dead,
asleep awhile in Jesus
their Lord and living Head.

How sweet their resurrection
when He shall bid them rise
to join the celebration
and to enjoy the Prize!

                    May, 2010

On the Death of Shell Regan

Snatched from the world at God's command,
Blameless and harmless now you stand,
Seeing the Majesty and Grace
That brought you near to His embrace.
Your earthly labors quickly done,
To stand and serve before God's Son,
Forever with your Jesus blest,
Forever tasting of His rest,
Now waiting for the final day
When heaven and earth shall pass away.
In Salem's towers your soul shall be
In joy and perfect liberty.
When God removes His dwelling here

In Sorrow and In Joy

To be to us forever near,
Our Deepest Joy and Great Reward
To be forever with our Lord.

> May, 2010

On Anderson Manor

In the Anderson Manor where history curls
Up the chimneys like smoke in soft, wispy, white whirls,
In the Anderson Manor where Time creeps the halls
Whisp'ring legends of gatherings, banquets, and balls,
The Past breathes its presence, the Future looms too,
A blink of an eye and a century's through.
You enter a stranger, perhaps from afar.
You leave as a relative, fam'ly you are.
So jot down this place in your personal planner.
You'll be treated, I know, in the Anderson manner.

> June, 2010

On the Sacrifice of Isaac

When You commanded Abraham
his well-loved son to slay,
You did not let him plunge the knife
but Isaac got away
because a ram, in wandering
was found within the place,
his horns caught in the thickets;
but yet, by wond'rous grace
You, Father, smote Your only Son
when He our burden bare
with justice to the utmost
and would not Jesus spare.
The ram was no more there by chance
than was the Son that day

when, hanging on the awful tree,
He bore our guilt away.
The patriarch's obedience
his other loves all paled,
So Your great love to all Your own
Your very Son impaled.
Your servant called the dreadful place
"Jehovah will provide"
because he knew that by Christ's death
we would be justified.
The promised Seed when truly come
the one and only Son,
by His own life and cruel death
salvation for us won.
What love was this that would not stay
Your hand when You Him slew?
Amazing Pity, Matchless Love,
towards us that hated You!

                June 2010

For the Deacons

Fast to the precious Truth
With unfeigned faith you cling,
Boldness your treasure be
In service of the King!
Gaining a good degree,
The greatest shall he be
Who images his Lord
In most humility.
Who bends himself most low,
For others spends his care,
In service shall he then
His Savior's image bear.

                July 2010

In Sorrow and In Joy

On the Death of S. L.

He went to work last weekend,
but yesterday he died.
His plans now all forgotten,
his hopes all petrified.
Without a hope of Glory,
without a Savior sure,
How awful is the prospect,
forever to endure
the wrath of God unceasing,
His angry rage unfurled,
and into it forever
his fearful soul is hurled.
How mighty is the Mercy
that saves a single soul,
forever ill-deserving
but graciously made whole!
I am not one bit better,
my sins are just as grim,
and were it not for Mercy,
I'd be in Hell like him.

      August 2010

Naomi

Back from an exile far away,
left of her sons and cov'nant head
with Ruth alone along the way
returning to the House of Bread.
Bearing in symbol all the curse
of Israel when she left her God,
hopeless and helpless, poor and weak,
evil the way that she had trod.

In Sorrow and In Joy

Coming back home at harvest time,
begging a pittance for their meal.
What could their poverty allay?
What could their grievous losses heal?
But then a righteous, godly man,
image of Him that was to come,
took Ruth to be his very own,
gave her a son and welcome home.
To the Most Bitter is a child
born that will ease her later years,
born that will bear her burden great,
born that will calm her constant fears.
O Blest Redeemer, praise to Thee
Who from the curse has ransomed me,
giving not only what I need
but Thine own self in very deed.

December 2010

Solitude

I have no husband and no child,
but yet I clearly see
the Mighty Mercy and the Grace
Thou hast bestowed on me.
For Thou hast given me Thyself,
more dear than all beside,
and promised me that, live or die,
I shall with Thee abide.
What joy has earth without Thee, Lord?
What pleasure could there be
if I had all that I could wish
but were bereft of Thee?

December 2010

Ravens

What can I lack if Thou provide?
How can I want for food?
Elijah was by ravens fed;
Thou didst command his good.

> January 2011

Sustained by a Widow

Thou didst command Thy servant
to Zarephath to go.
A widow would sustain him;
he would provision know.
"Make me thereof a cake first
and then for yours and you."
She heard his word and harkened—
God's Word could not fall through.
In Heaven He saw and noticed.
He saw His own obey.
He made the meal sufficient
until the final day.
The flour did not falter,
the oil did not cease,
until the rains from heaven
upon the earth released.
Whatever He has promised
He's able to provide.
And safe shall be all people
that do in Him confide.

> January 2011

In Sorrow and In Joy

From Proverbs 31

Who can a godly woman find?
Than precious stones more rare . . .
Her spouse may trust her with his goods
For spoils he need not care.
She does him good through all her days;
She works with willing hands.
She brings provisions from afar,
Her food from distant lands.
She rises also in the night,
For hers, she food prepares.
Astute in business,
Hard at work, she labors at her wares.
She girds herself with strength about,
Her arm she strengthens too,
She sees that what she does is good,
Her labors are not few.
She works by day and in the night,
Her hands are skilled to sew.
She spins and weaves the flax herself,
The distaffs her hands know.
Her hand unto the poor is stretched,
The needy feel her touch.
She cares for all her household's needs,
The snow she fears not much.
Her garments are of linen fine,
In purple she is garbed,
But on her tongue is kindness, for
No word of hers is barbed.
She is not lazy, no, not she,
As all her children know
And rise at last to honor her
And all her graces show.
Though many favor beauty fine,

And others charm extol,
Yet she who fears the Lord shall be
More beautiful than all.

February 2011

From Romans 15

Though there is One Who had a right
To please Himself in every way,
He laid aside prerogatives
To serve His people on that day.
Though He was strong, since we were weak,
He did not hesitate at all
To bear our weakness in Himself,
To raise us from our tragic Fall.
Though He was rich, since we are poor,
He laid aside His wealth and state
To take our poverty on Him
And give to us His riches great.
Though He was well, since we were ill,
He took our syndromes as His own,
He took up our infirmities
When He came from His lofty throne.
How dare I then look at my friends,
Those who my brethren are this day,
Think them unworthy of the cost
He paid Who bore my sins away?
So let me cheer the saddest soul,
And let me spend whate'er it be
That I may lift up him who falls
As He Himself has rescued me.

February 2011

On Human Opinion

I see you think not much of me—
You see my sins are not a few,
But if you knew what's in my heart
You'd think much worse than now you do.

      March 2011

To Our Lord, Jesus Christ

Mine were the thorns, the nakedness and shame.
Yours was the crown, the modesty, the fame.
Mine was the curse, the awful death, the pain.
Yours was the blessing, life, and blissful gain.
How could You bear my dreadful death for me?
O unmatched love of Yours that could not be
Except it reunite Your own with You,
Take all our falsehood and return us True!
Not the first Cov'nant Head in all our place,
But better than our father first You are
Not driving us from our great God away
But bringing us. Your chosen, from afar.

      March 2011

On the Anger of Jesus Christ

Lord, loose Your righteous outrage
On death's destructive power,
As You of old were angry
To see its dreadful hour.
Mankind is so besotten,
So miserable and poor,
Thus, moved with great compassion,
O be our Savior sure.

In Sorrow and In Joy

Have mercy on us, Jesus,
As only You can do
And free us from sin's bondage,
That we may dwell with You.

March 2011

Dust

It comforts me that You are there
Since I my weakness owned.
Beside the Majesty on high,
Earth's dust is now enthroned.

March 2011

A Secret Princess

(For the Young Daughters of the King)

I am a secret princess,
Although no one might guess.
I don't live in a palace
Or have a fancy dress.
I don't have lots of servants
Or sit upon a throne,
But still I am a princess,
I am my Savior's own.
A child of heaven unnoticed
By most the world, you see,
But when He comes in glory,
A princess I shall be.
Obscurity my mantle,
In this the present hour,
But bright shall be my raiment
When He appears in power.

In Sorrow and In Joy

So let the world despise me
And think my worth so small.
When He shall come triumphant,
I will not care at all.

April 2011

In Contemplation of a Dying Saint

We do not die as others do,
Bereft of hope or cheer,
Because our Father holds us close
As to His throne we near.
It is not chance that ends our days:
It is His plan and will.
We live as long as He ordained
And rest upon Him still.
Therefore we do not fear our death:
It brings us to His throne.
As He ordained we first were born,
And then were called His own,
So He will take us home with Him
When He deems it is right.
To Him, the dying saint is dear,
His people His delight.
So, come, Sweet Death and take me home
Upon the purposed day.
I long to see His face at last
And would no longer stay.

May 2011

In Sorrow and In Joy

For Jack, on the Occasion of His Death

Now you are free at last,
Not as the world might say,
Free from your sins and fears
Free from your sad decay.
Free in your Savior's love,
Forevermore to rest,
Seeing His Glorious Face,
Leaning upon His breast.
Blest be His tender love
That snatched you from the flame,
Restored your voice at last,
To bless His Holy Name.
From tribulation free,
Washed in the precious flow
That makes us sinners vile
To be as white as snow.
You did not cease to be
As some state foolishly.
This is no childhood tale—
Heav'n is reality.

May 2011

For Marjorie Paauwe, on the Occasion of Her Death

(From Revelation 14: Contrasting the end of the World and the end of the Christian)

The Lamb stands on the mount,
His faithful foll'wers true,
His army clad in white,
His virgin retinue,

In Sorrow and In Joy

They wait upon His will,
They follow His command,
They haste o'er sea and plain
Or over desert land.
The song they sing is new,
Unheard on earth before,
As many waters loud,
As many oceans' roar,
No one can learn that song
But those snatched from the flame,
No one can say those words
But those that love the Name.
The Harlot is destroyed,
Great Babylon did fall,
Our God has overcome
Those who opposed Him all.
'Tis time for grace and wrath
To meet at Judgment Hall,
Some to behold His face,
Some by His anger fall.
Though Hell be fired hot
and multitudes be burned
all are by Mercy saved
that to the Savior turned.
Not good in their own selves
Nor righteous on their own
But hid in Christ their Lord,
All safe before the Throne.
Blessed are the holy dead
That died in Christ before.
Their eyes shall but behold
The burning of the whore.
The world is passed away,
The glad Eternal come;
The Christian rests at last

In Sorrow and In Joy

In her familial home.
The earthly swept away
Before the judgment wave,
The righteous hid in Christ
Are rescued from the grave.
She shall arise again
In youth and vigor free,
She shall enjoy the Prize
In Heaven's family.

June 2011

For a Pharisee, in Contemplation of Her Death

Full of yourself and pride,
Righteous in your own mind,
What has death brought to you?
What did you grieving find?
Was your own list of rules
Good enough for His eye?
Was your false piety
Suited for Him to try?
Not caring for His own,
Nor loving Him at all,
Where is your boasting now?
Did you arise or fall?
He sought for mercy kind
And justice pure and true.
Tell me, O Pharisee,
Did He find them in you?

June 2011

In Sorrow and In Joy

On Being a Woman

Don't say I am a poet:
To that I won't confess.
In case you didn't know it,
I am a poetess.

June 2011

Death's Invitation

Come and lie down, lie down, lie down,
Lie down, my dear, and sleep.
Tis time to rest until the Dawn;
There's no more time to weep.
The former things are passed away,
The true Eternal come
Rest from your journey, weary one,
You are at last at home.

June 2011

Another Take on Childhood Songs: Jesus Loves Me

Jesus loves me, this I know,
For the Bible tells me so.
His elect to Him belong
They are weak, but He is strong.

June 2011

In Sorrow and In Joy

Another Take on Childhood Songs: Jesus Loves the Little Children

Jesus loves His chosen people,
All His people in the world,
Red and yellow, black and white
They are precious in His sight.
Jesus loves His chosen people in the world.
Jesus died for all His people,
All His people in the world,
Red and yellow, black and white,
They are precious in His sight.
Jesus died for all His people in the world.

June 2011

Blind Bartimaeus

I heard that You were passing by
Though You I could not see.
I knew that only David's Son
Could heal and rescue me.
I cried aloud: they were not pleased
And bade me to be still;
I was determined to be healed
If it should be Your will.
You stopped and called me to Yourself,
I cast my rags away
And came at once to bow myself
And at Your feet to pray.
I have no other Hope or Help,
So grievous is my sore,
If You do not have mercy, Lord,
I have no rescue more.
You spoke the Word of pow'r to me

My eyes were opened wide.
I could not go away with joy
But followed at Your side.
No blindness is as great as that
Which cannot clearly see
Christ Jesus is man's only hope:
None other could there be.

June 2011

From Numbers 16

Against You we had sinned
Rebelled and disobeyed,
Your anger was so hot,
Your hand was then unstayed.
Our Surety intervened.
To bear Your wrath His hap,
He offered up Himself;
He stood within the gap.
He took on Him our sins
Our covenantal Head,
His prayers stood between
The living and the dead.
Blest be the Mercy great
That gave our Christ to be
Both Priest and Sacrifice
For all eternity.

June 2011

In Sorrow and In Joy

From Exodus 33 and Romans 3

We fell short of the mark,
we did not hit the goal.
We failed to obey,
we injured each his soul.
Your anger grew so hot,
Your Glory shone so fair
it would have burned us up
if gazing we should dare.
You hid us in the Rock,
our covering Your hand,
You passed by and declared
Your Goodness sweet and grand.
You hid us from Yourself,
lest we should be consumed.
Your took our debt on You,
our trespass You assumed.
You gave us righteousness
that would withstand Your eye.
Your bore our penalty,
for we deserved to die.
What grace is this that gives
life where death's merited?
It was not earned by us.
It was inherited.

                    June 2011

My Burka

I have a secret burka
which no one else can see.
It covers me from head to toe:
its name is Modesty.
You won't find me without it;

In Sorrow and In Joy

I will not be exposed,
except with my own husband
behind a door that's closed.

                    June 2011

The Command
(Ephesians 5:18–20)

You gave us a command:
an order from our King:
You bade us to be glad,
to celebrate and sing.
How could we silent be,
refuse to render praise
for Mercy and for Grace
that gladden all our days?

                    June 2011

On the Refusal of a Friend to Repent

You would not warning hear,
refusing to repent.
You would not be ashamed;
your heart would not relent.
You would retain your sin
nor cast it far away.
You would not hear the Word,
refusing to obey.
What was it worth to you?
And why not bow the knee?
Is your pride worth the price—
death for eternity?
A certain fire shall burn
by Justice lit this flame,

it will consume all those
that hate the Sacred Name.
If after we have heard
we trespass willfully
no sacrifice remains,
just Hell eternally.
You can't escape this fate
pretending it's not there.
If you will not repent,
beware, my friend, beware.

>   July 2011

"But With Most of Them, He was not Well-Pleased"

But forty days had passed,
so hard Your people fell,
they made them idol gods,
forgot Your grace as well.
They built a golden calf
before it bowed to pray,
forgetting Him that lead
them through the Red Sea way.
Your anger burned so hot,
Your hand You did not stay,
for twenty thousand plus
fell on a single day.
Not all that 'scaped their bonds
arrived in peace at last:
most fell beside the way,
consumed by anger's blast.
So therefore, let us fear
lest we should seem to fail,
to fall upon the way,

and not by faith prevail.
While it is called "today,"
let us forsake our sin.
Let us to heaven attain,
he that endures shall win.

    July 2011

On the Death of Gabriella Valente

So young and fair a child,
so quickly snatched away—
gone from this realm of sin
gone to a brighter day.
So young to join the throng
around the Throne on high,
So young to cease from sin,
so young indeed to die.
Not an untimely death,
but in His plan and will,
no more to live on earth,
but gone to serve Him still.
Saved from the ravages
of life not meant to be,
gone home to heav'n to rest,
rest for eternity.
Safe in your Savior's arms,
perfect in heart and soul,
ravaged by vicious Death,
but by His grace made whole.
Worshipping without stain,
by Death you ceased from sin,
to heav'n's eternal bliss,
through Death you entered in.

    July 2011

In Sorrow and In Joy

Dwelling in Tents With Abraham, Isaac, and Jacob

I have no home of brick,
nor yet a house of stone,
This body is a tent
though it is not my own.
And He shall fold it up,
not that I shall return
from whence I journeyed forth,
the city that shall burn.
Then do not tempt my soul
with trinkets foul or fair,
I have no treasure here;
my home is over there
where He sits on the throne;
of me, He's not ashamed;
and I shall see His face
who by His Grace He claimed.

August, 2011

On Yet Another Average Review

I worked so hard and long
I spent my strength and health,
I got a tiny raise
that won't increase my wealth.
But there is only One
Who always did His best,
Who never slacked at all,
Who never failed the test.
And He shall be the judge
Who shall the case review,

and I will leave my cause,
my Righteous Lord, with You.

                August 2011

On The Prayed For Conversion of a Friend

You have an arm of flesh,
a weakness so profound.
You cannot save yourself
or turn yourself around.
A deadness in your soul
which cannot even hear
the Gospel when it sounds
upon your outward ear.
But there is Strength and Might
in Him who reigns above,
Whose arm can raise the dead,
Whose covenantal love
His own has set apart.
And with almighty power
He can convert your soul
At His appointed hour.
Therefore I can be glad
have confidence and joy
For He Who reigns above
my weakness can deploy,
my falt'ring witness bless,
my halting speech improve
to raise you from the dead
through His almighty love.

                August 2011

In Sorrow and In Joy

On My Nephew's Wedding

(I Thessalonians 3:8)

One of the blessings great
God's people often see
besides their God by faith
is their posterity.
A child becomes a man,
He takes himself a bride
a helpmeet fit for him
to walk along beside.
Then come the little ones
with promise good and sweet,
a promise of good things
which hopefully they meet.
I have no child to see
a husband take or wife:
I have no life on earth
beyond my mortal life
But yet there is a home
and family more near,
the family of God,
than relatives more dear.
If that should healthy be
and grow and prosper still,
it is enough for me,
my deepest longings fill.
If Christ should find His church,
His wife in readiness,
it will content my soul:
I have contentedness.

August 2011

God is a Man of War

God is a man of war:
of righteousness profound,
of justice pure and high,
Who will His foes confound.
How can it be that we
have peace with Him above?
Our sins His judgment earned
and forfeited His love.
But He unleashed His Wrath,
His fiery Anger hot,
against His very Son
and spared our Jesus not.
He poured out all His Rage,
He made War on His Son,
He cast His soul to Hell,
His own Beloved One.
And then He raised Him up,
for now our Jesus lives,
and to the ones He loves
His very self He gives.
How can we then be still
at such amazing grace
and not return our thanks
before His Blessed Face?

August 2011

Resurrection

Not to the wise and great
did You Your vict'ry show
when risen from the grave
but to a woman low.
Not to a teacher great
or master high and grand,

In Sorrow and In Joy

> but to the Magdalene
> You rescued by Your hand.
> Because she loved You much
> for Mercies great and free,
> for he who loves You much
> shall Your sweet presence see.
> Salvation's not by works,
> but yet works cannot fail,
> not our works but Your own,
> that can alone avail.
> Obedient unto death,
> which we could never be,
> and vindicated raised
> for all eternity.
>
> September 2011

On "One Ocean," a Song Heard at Sea World®

Our hope is not ecology
nor aught that sinners do.
Our only Hope is Jesus Christ,
the Man from Heaven True.
For Adam brought nor joy nor hope
but misery and pain,
but earth shall have its Sabbaths
when the Christ returns again.
For God this earth shall form again,
man's refuse all destroy.
The Second Man's our only Hope,
our one eternal Joy.
There shall indeed be just one song
with which the earth shall ring.
It shall be "Hallelujah!" to our God,
of kings the King.

September 2011

In Sorrow and In Joy

On Psalm 8, Hebrews 2, and Sea World®

You put beneath man's feet
all things that fly or swim;
all things that creep or crawl,
they homage give to him.
Not yet to him we see
obedient each thing,
but we see Jesus Christ,
already crowned the King,
Who shall His sceptre sway
o'er earth from sea to sea.
All things shall Him obey
in perfect harmony.
They shall not hurt or kill
in all Your dwelling place,
for man renewed shall live
before Your Blessed Face.

                    September 2011

On Luke 16

Tell me, you who treasure riches,
who in fact was more secure—
the proud, rich man in his palace
or the beggar at his door?

                    September 2011

In Sorrow and In Joy

Ambition

From Ecclesiastes 7:27–28
If you ask me my ambition,
this is what I have in mind:
I should like to be the woman
that the Preacher could not find.

September 2011

Comfort

From II Corinthians 1:3

God be blessed, Who in our woe
grants that we may comfort know
so that we may comfort those
who are pained with other woes.

September 2011

Two Hands

My hand that grasps my God
is feeble, weak, and poor,
But there's another hand
that holds my soul secure.
Though my poor grasp may slip
and through my weakness fail,
the hand of God Almighty
forever will prevail.

September 2011

In Sorrow and In Joy

On Seeing a Rainbow

High in the heav'ns You hung Your bow,
Your wat'ry weapon great,
with which You smote the ancient world
and made it desolate.
And with the eight you saved from death
and every bird and beast
You cov'nant made You'd no more drown
the world from West to East.
The sunlight shines through rain and cloud
as through a prism fair
which breaks the light in colors bright
to sparkle in the air.
Of faithful cov'nant the sign,
stretched far across the sky.
Our science may hint at what You do,
but Scripture tells us why.

                    September 2011

Welcome to the Church

Come, all you weak, come all you poor,
come all you sick and troubled sore,
come to the table Grace has set,
come, fallen, to the safety net.
Come taste the Feast the poor may eat;
come taste the Strength the weak find sweet.
Sit at the Gospel's mighty board:
come to the Church of Christ the Lord.
No Pharisee need venture nigh,
no man that thinks himself so high;
the righteous need not travel here
for sinners only may appear

to take the mercy freely given,
to feel before the joy of heaven.
Come with your debts unto His wealth,
come change your sickness for His health.
Come, sinners to the God of Grace,
come be found pure before His face.
Come with true penitence and grief
to find in Christ your sure relief.
You have no need He can't supply.
Your souls His grace can justify.
You shall be clean as driven snow
who shall His grace and mercy know.

October 2011

Grace is a Flower

Grace is a flower, wondrous fair,
that spreads its sweetness through the air.
So delicate this plant, you know,
on Adam's soil it will not grow.
If you should find it blooming here,
you know what Gardener was near.

October 2011

A Man of Sorrows

He, Who should have had great joy,
peace, delight, and bright tomorrows
had instead our deep distress
and was called the Man of Sorrows.

October 2011

In Sorrow and In Joy

Three Shipwrecks

From II Corinthians 11

Was God so angry with poor Paul
He tossed him three times in the drink?
Three shipwrecks. Not a punishment
But blessing towards His own, I think.

                    October 2011

Mary and Martha

Martha would bid Mary serve
Upon a busy day,
But from her who would hear Your Word
You would not take away
The thing she valued most of all
And bade Your handmaid stay.

                    October 2011

Why?

Mercy's heaped on us below
So that praise may upward go.

                    October 2011

Jericho

(The King mounts His assault on the hearts of men
in an apartment complex in Jacksonville, Florida)

Lord, march about these battlements
and shout aloud Your grace.
O flatten all these fortresses
before Your Blessed Face.

In Sorrow and In Joy

Not as of old in judgment
but in Your gracious will,
make these to call upon You
and Your decree fulfill.
Have mercy on these sinners
as on us You have had,
and by Your mercy make them
with us exceeding glad.
Lord, save these sinners with us
as only You can do.
We look for saving power
for these poor sinners few.
You have an arm almighty
which no man can withstand.
You will save all Your people
by Your almighty hand.

October 2011

On the Marriage of Two Friends

I prayed for each of you
that my God would provide
a godly spouse and true
that would with you abide.
And see, this blessed day
God's mercy's waterfall
from heaven streaming down
and drenching one and all!
Grace, matchless, great, and free
bestowed by Endless Love,
to urge you on towards home
in His abode above.

October 2011

In Sorrow and In Joy

On a Couple Being Reunited in Marriage
(From John 3:29 and Joel 2:25)

He stands and hears his voice:
the bridegroom's joy resounds.
His friend is full of joy.
His gladness knows no bounds.
Blessed be the God of Grace
Who reunites this day
a couple that was split
To walk along the way.
The canker ate so much,
The locust grain destroyed,
but God restores the loss,
with gladness unalloyed.
New woman and new man,
new family of Grace,
that shall His Mercy know
and see His Blessed Face.

                December 2011

On Christian Liberty

He bled for you. He died.
They mocked at Him. They spat.
How can I then demand
my right to this or that
I feel I want to eat
or drink or see or do
despite the fact it may
destroy or humble you?
I would prefer to starve,
have nothing for my meal,
than damage you my friend

because His love I feel.
For I would rather die
than make you, friend, to fall.
Because I love your soul,
I would forego it all.

December 2011

I John 4:7-8

If I love Him then you
are most beloved too.
If I'm not moved by love,
I'm not born from above.

December 2011

Ambition II

O Herod, how much evil
was in you, but not good!
You would have killed the Christ child,
our Savior, if you could.
Our Hope and Consolation,
our one eternal Joy,
But you would have Him murdered
when He was but a boy.

December 2011

www.ingramcontent.com/pod-product-compliance
Lightning Source LLC
Chambersburg PA
CBHW070501090426
42735CB00012B/2642